TOMATO AND CUCUMBER GROWING FOR PROFIT

BY

J. W. MORTON, F.R.H.S., F.N.I.A.B.

PAST PRESIDENT OF THE MARCH AND DISTRICT
FRUITGROWERS' AND NURSERYMEN'S ASSOCIATION

MEMBER OF THE COMMITTEE OF THE WISBECH
AND DISTRICT FRUITGROWERS' AND NURSERY-
MEN'S ASSOCIATION

R.H.S. TEACHERS' CERTIFICATE IN HORTICULTURE

Copyright © 2013 Read Books Ltd.
This book is copyright and may not be
reproduced or copied in any way without
the express permission of the publisher in writing

British Library Cataloguing-in-Publication Data
A catalogue record for this book is available from the
British Library

Vegetable Growing at Home

(Kitchen Garden)

Whether you have a massive plot, or just a few planters, growing vegetables is satisfying as well as healthy. It also has a long history, dating back to French Renaissance 'potagers' and Victorian Kitchen gardens. Kitchen gardens in turn have emerged from the 'Cottage Garden', the earliest of which were much more practical than their modem descendants. These were working class gardens, with an emphasis on vegetables and herbs, along with some fruit trees, perhaps a beehive and even livestock, with flowers only used to fill any spaces in-between. The traditional potager / kitchen garden, also known in Scotland as a 'kailyaird', is a space separate from the rest of the residential garden, possessing a different history as well as design, from traditional 'family farm' plots.

The kitchen garden may serve as the central feature of an ornamental, all-season landscape, or it may be little more than a humble vegetable plot. It is a source of herbs, vegetables and fruits, but it is often also a structured garden space, sometimes incorporating beautiful geometric designs. The historical design precedent is from the Gardens of the French Renaissance and Baroque Garden à la française eras, where flowers (edible and non-edible) and herbs were planted alongside vegetables to enhance the garden's beauty. More common in the UK however, are simpler 'vegetable gardens' (also known as patches or plots), which exist purely to grow vegetables – aside from any aesthetic purpose. It will typically include a compost heap and several plots of divided areas of land, intended to grow one or two types of plant in each plot. These plots are ordinarily divided into rows, with an assortment of vegetables grown in the different lines.

With worsening economic conditions and increased interest in organic and sustainable living, many people are turning to vegetable gardening as a supplement to their family's diet. Food grown in the back yard consumes little if any fuel for shipping or maintenance, and the grower can be sure of what exactly was used to grow it. Such means of organic gardening have become increasingly popular for the modern home gardener, and fit in with broader trends towards sustainability and 'permaculture.' Through each person using the land and resources available to them, the home vegetable-grower has perhaps unwittingly become a part of this movement; a branch of ecological design and engineering, that develops sustainable, self-maintaining agricultural systems. The term originally referred to 'permanent agriculture' but was expanded to stand also for 'permanent culture', as it was seen that social aspects were integral to a truly sustainable system.

Permaculture's core tenets revolve around care for the earth, care for the people and return of surplus; a key element is maximising useful connections between the various components, and synergy of the final design. This may sound hard to achieve, but by making and storing one's own foodstuffs, this helps to minimise waste, human labour and energy input – you have already started! Frequently, when growing vegetables in the domestic gardens, 'herb gardens' will play a large part; they are normally purely functional, although many also arrange and clip the plants into ornamental patterns. Such herbs are used to flavour food in cooking, though they may also be used in other ways, such as discouraging pests, providing pleasant scents, or serving medicinal purposes (such as a physic garden), among others. Many herbs also grow well in pots / containers, giving the kitchen gardener the added benefit of mobility. Mint is an especially good example of a herb advisable to keep in a container – or its roots take over the whole garden.

Some of the easiest vegetables to grow are French beans; easy to sow and don't need support, so are easy to tend. Peas too are fantastic, as well as being fun to harvest for children. Beetroots, courgettes and lettuces are also good vegetables for beginners. The widespread uses, practical as well as edible, make vegetables a perfect thing to grow at home; and dependent on location and climate – they can be very low-maintenance crops. Even though technically a fruit, growing one's own fresh, juicy tomatoes is one of the great pleasures of summer gardening, and if the gardener doesn't have much room, hanging baskets are a good solution. The types, methods and approaches to growing vegetables are myriad, and far too numerous to be discussed in any detail here in this introduction, but there are always easy ways to get started for the complete novice. We hope that the reader is inspired by this book on vegetables and kitchen gardens – and is encouraged to start, or continue their own cultivations. Good Luck!

PREFACE

In writing this work the author has tried to make it as practical and as useful as possible. It has been his aim to avoid personal opinions and to rely upon practice that has been tried and proved in the business time after time.

That there is room for extension of tomato and cucumber growing under present trade conditions without overcrowding is too well known to need repeating. Indeed an increased home production is a necessity, and it is the duty of the grower to supply that necessity.

If the experienced grower finds this book a reliable work of reference and the grower with less experience finds it a reliable guide to successful cultivation, the author will feel that his work has not been in vain.

To any of the younger generation who wish to enter the industry, we would impress the necessity for thoroughness and cleanliness. These two

6   *Preface*

qualities are essential if success in commercial growing with these crops is desired, and given them the young grower will be well equipped for the industry in question.

THE AUTHOR.

CONTENTS

		PAGE
PREFACE	. . . .	5

TOMATOES

CHAP.		
I.	CHOICE OF SITE. TYPE OF HOUSE. VARIETIES	9
II.	THE SOIL	13
III.	PROPAGATION. POTTING. PLANTING .	14
IV.	POTS AND BOXES	21
V.	CARE AFTER PLANTING. MULCHING. TRIMMING. WEIGHT OF CROP . . .	23
VI.	GATHERING AND MARKETING. GRADING. PACKING	27
VII.	DISEASES OF TOMATOES	30
VIII.	PESTS	37

CUCUMBERS

IX.	SITE. PROPAGATION. VARIETIES . .	45
X.	PREPARATION AND PLANTING. CLEANING .	48
XI.	CARE AFTER PLANTING. TRIMMING, TRAINING AND STOPPING	51
XII.	GATHERING AND MARKETING . . .	54
XIII.	PESTS AND DISEASES	56
XIV.	OUTDOOR TOMATOES AND RIDGE CUCUMBERS	60

TOMATOES

CHAPTER I

CHOICE OF SITE

PREPARATION for the cultivation of tomatoes on a commercial scale needs careful thought. The greater the amount of care that is exercised at this stage the greater will be the possibilities of success.

The selection of a suitable position is important. Although in most cases it will be necessary to select a site from a limited number of pieces of land available, it is nevertheless advisable to have an idea as to what is wanted, so that one may approach as near to the most favourable conditions as possible.

Although a slight slope is favoured by some growers, there is no doubt that a level well-drained situation is on the whole more suitable; natural drainage being preferable to the use of pipes or other methods; but whatever method is employed, thorough drainage will be necessary.

Depth of soil is another important point which cannot be ignored. Although tomatoes may be grown successfully on a wide range of soils, they will not do well where the soil is only shallow. They must have a good depth of soil if good results are to be obtained.

Tomato Growing for Profit

Situation is a matter of greater importance than is generally realised. There must be a plentiful supply of clean water; lack of this will be fatal. It it also advisable to be within a reasonable distance of a railway, and if not too far from a market so much the better, as transport costs are an important factor with a crop of this kind.

Although tomatoes will grow on a wide range of soils, it would be as well before going further to name those that are most suitable. A good deep loam is probably preferable to any other kind, while a sandy loam is excellent. Heavy soils can be improved by the addition of ashes, burnt earth, good clean manure from the farmyard or stable, but care should be taken that the animals have been carefully fed or the manure may prove more trouble than benefit.

It is important that with new land devoted to this crop, freedom from soil pests should be assured. In some of the most favourable soils wireworm may be found, and it will be necessary to entirely clear the land of these before any attempt is made at tomato growing. The best way to do this is by means of an efficient soil insecticide. In any case it is essential that the land should be free from pests of this kind.

TYPE OF HOUSE

The type of house is a matter which will need to be decided. Here it will be for the grower to

Tomato Growing for Profit

decide for himself. Growers of long experience have different ideas as to the most suitable type, and the favourite design with one grower will not be the favourite with another.

A type that is favoured by a large number of experienced growers is what is known as the aeroplane. This house is about fourteen or fifteen feet wide with the gutters about six or seven feet from the ground.

The houses should run from north to south if at all possible.

It must be repeated, however, that many success-ful growers favour other types of houses.

It may be stressed again that there must be perfect cleanliness everywhere. Clean soil, plenty of pure air, clean water in abundance must be available, and the houses, both paint and glass, must be kept perfectly clean, otherwise the difficulties which the grower will have to face will be greatly increased.

VARIETIES

The variety to be grown is a matter of considerable importance. Some varieties which are excellent from the cropping point of view may be rather clumsy in appearance, other varieties are suitable for the early market.

The qualities to look for in the selection of varieties are short-jointed plants of vigorous habit of growth which produce nicely-shaped well-coloured fruits with a good number of fruits to a truss.

Tomato Growing for Profit

It is always a good plan to follow the example of successful growers in the neighbourhood, and to plant varieties that have proved successful in their case. It should be remembered that with tomatoes as with most other products of the soil, the quality favoured by the public varies to some extent in different districts, and it is always as well to cater for the needs of the public.

It is usually a bad plan to try experiments with new varieties except on a very small scale. Tried and proved varieties will be the most satisfactory in the long run, but the seed must be obtained from a really reliable firm and should be taken from plants entirely free from mosaic.

A few among several varieties that have proved themselves of value are Carter's Sunrise, Kondine Red, Market King, Ailsa Craig, Nonsuch, Best of All.

Of these Ailsa Craig is a first-class variety possessing all the qualities of a commercial tomato, including that of heavy cropping. Kondine Red is also a favourite, perhaps the favourite, with many commercial growers, but the quality does not appeal to us as being quite equal to some of the other varieties mentioned.

There is one other point in the selection of varieties that the grower cannot afford to neglect. Disease may cause serious loss in the tomato house, and certain varieties are more subject to disease than are others. Other things being equal, it is as

Tomato Growing for Profit

well to select a variety which is to some extent disease resisting, so that any chance of loss from this cause is reduced to a minimum.

CHAPTER II

THE SOIL

IF a succession of good crops is to be obtained year after year, the soil will need a great deal of consideration and care.

It is almost impossible to keep the yield up to the standard of the first few years, but the falling off should be as slight as possible, and it is largely a matter of soil treatment which will counteract the effect of constant cropping on the same soil.

There is no doubt as to the benefits which are derived from sterilisation, in fact this treatment is a necessity. The question as to the method of sterilisation is one which will need to be decided.

The two methods regularly used are steam sterilisation and sterilisation by means of chemicals. Each has certain advantages, but it is probable that by employing both methods during different seasons the most satisfactory results will be obtained.

Steam sterilisation has a good deal to recommend it, but it has a tendency to make the soil very dry indeed, and in addition it is rather expensive. Usually it is not necessary to sterilise by means of steam more often than every other year.

Steam sterilisation renders the soil entirely free

14 *Tomato Growing for Profit*

from pests, and in this respect it has the advantage of most other forms; but in order to employ this method, proper sterilising apparatus should be used to make sure that it is done thoroughly, and it is this apparatus that is expensive.

It has the advantage of rendering many plant foods in the soil more easy of access.

Sometimes the method of baking the soil is practised, but this is a rather slow process when any quantity of soil has to be dealt with and is not as effective as steaming.

Soil-sterilising liquids are placed on the market, and if obtained from a reliable firm, these may be used with every confidence. These liquids are watered in thoroughly. When purchasing sterilisers of this type the directions should be followed as exactly as possible. If no directions are given, these should be obtained from the firm. It is unfortunate that it does sometimes happen that horticultural firms supply spraying and sterilising materials without including directions for their use. This is not of much importance when these are supplied to experienced growers, but when they go to those who are inexperienced it is a matter of some importance.

CHAPTER III

PROPAGATION

THE usual and best method of propagating tomatoes for the commercial grower is from seed.

Tomato Growing for Profit

We may repeat here that a good foundation is the keynote of success, and it will pay the grower to take a good deal of trouble to ensure a good plant.

A propagating house is a big advantage, and unless there is any very special reason for doing without one of these, it is almost a necessity. Almost, but not altogether, for several growers in a small way of business known to me manage very successfully without the aid of a propagating house. Nevertheless, the grower will feel the benefit of such a house in many ways.

The period during which seed may be sown varies a good deal, and is dependent upon the time that it is desired to harvest the crop. Mid-winter is a favourite time, but November sowing is also largely practised, as-is sowing well on into the new year. The district in which the grower is situated will also make a big difference as to the most suitable time to sow the seed.

The soil in which seed is sown must be fresh, or if this is not possible it should be sterilised.

It is impossible to be too particular upon a matter of this kind, as the whole success of the sowing may depend upon the fact that the soil is in good condition.

If chemicals are used for sterilising the soil, this should be done some time beforehand.

Growers in different parts of the country have different methods of seed sowing. The fact that success follows several different methods proves

16 Tomato Growing for Profit

that there is no need for any hard-and-fast rules. A common method is to sow in seed boxes. The soil used at the bottom of the seed box may with advantage be somewhat coarser than that used for the top, but the layer of rather coarse soil should be thin and is used in order to assist drainage. When sufficient soil has been placed in the boxes, this is levelled and slightly pressed.

Tomato seed should be very thinly sown. This is a point which many experienced growers appear to ignore, but there will be much better prospect of a high percentage of really sturdy plants if thin sowing is rigidly adhered to.

It is possible that success will follow thick sowing, but it is certainly not the best method and is not recommended. On the other hand, there is no need for the careful spacing out of each seed a certain distance from its neighbour. This is going to the other extreme and is a waste of both time and labour.

When the seed is sown, a small quantity of soil is sifted over it through a very fine sieve.

After sowing, the seed box is watered through a fine rose and covered with glass.

The seed used should be obtained from a reliable firm, and it is particularly important that no seed should be used from plants in a house in which there has been any sign of mosaic disease.

The temperature is an important matter. This should be kept within the limits of from sixty to sixty-five degrees. It should certainly not be

Tomato Growing for Profit

allowed to drop more than one or two degrees below this, although at the other end a little more latitude may be allowed.

The young plants should on no account be placed in such a position that they are drawn by the glass, as this will render them long, straggly and useless. It will be necessary to raise the glass over the boxes gradually as the plants grow.

The next important step in the work of the season is that of transferring the young plants to small pots. This is usually done when the plants attain the second pair of leaves.

POTTING

The work of potting should be just as carefully carried out as that of sowing the seed. The pots should be clean. Perhaps growers are at times a little careless in this respect, but there is always danger where there is lack of cleanliness with the tomato crop.

As is the case with soil used in the seed boxes, the soil used in the pots should be prepared about three weeks before it is wanted for use. Sterilisation is again a necessity, and even if the soil is fresh it is an advantage.

In preparing the soil it is an advantage to mix about a forty-eight pot of bone flour with each barrow-load of soil. The quantity of bone flour may be varied to some extent according to the kind of soil available.

The box of seedlings should be well watered about twenty-four hours before the young plants are lifted.

Clean crocks should be used at the bottom of the pots for drainage purposes. The young plants should be buried almost to the top of the seed leaves when planted.

The size of the pots used varies a good deal in the trade. For very early work thumb pots are at times used, but for general purposes two-and-a-half to three-inch pots are usually used.

After planting no water should be used for about twenty-four hours, when the plants may again be well watered.

Correct depth to plant Seedling Tomato: to the first pair of leaflets.

Watering is indeed a matter of considerable importance. The plants should never be allowed to remain in a sodden state. They should be allowed to get dry before being watered, but when watered, the watering should be very thorough.

On sunny days a little air may be admitted to the plants; the amount may be increased as growth continues.

When first potted, the plants may be allowed to

stand on the staging pot thick, but as they grow they should be spaced out to some extent.

PLANTING

When the plants reach a height of from six to eight inches they will be ready for planting out. It will be necessary, however, to make thorough preparation for this. It is usually only for early crops that pot culture is practised; for the main crop as well as for late crops the method of planting in the soil provided in the houses will vary to some extent with the type of house. The main consideration will be to allow the plants ample space for development and production, and at the same time to make the best possible use of all available space.

Ready to go in permanent position, about 8 inches high.

The minimum space that should be allowed is about two and a half square feet per plant. In large houses it is more or less the general practice to plant across the house, but this method is not always followed.

A usual distance for the rows apart is two feet,

20 *Tomato Growing for Profit*

with the plants from fifteen to eighteen inches apart in the rows.

Two important matters will need attention before any effort is made to put the young plants in the borders. The first is that of moisture. From a fortnight to three weeks before planting it will be necessary to give the borders one or more thorough waterings. This should on no account be done less than two clear weeks before it is intended to plant.

It is important also to remember that soil temperature is just as important, if not more so, than air temperature in the houses. In order to be certain that the plants will not receive a check through being placed in cold soil, it will be necessary to have the fires burning a week or so before it is intended to do any planting.

After the soil has been worked it will need treading down or otherwise firming. The amount of treading needed will vary with the soil, but with few exceptions, the chief exception being where the soil is very heavy, it will be advisable to tread down as firmly as possible ; in the case of very heavy soils it may not be advisable to tread down at all.

The preparation is now completed and the borders are ready for the plants.

Holes for the plants may be made with either trowel or dibber. There is a considerable difference of opinion among growers as to which of these tools is the most useful. In our opinion it is not

Tomato Growing for Profit 21

material which method is used so long as the holes are made with sufficient care to serve their purpose.

In turning the plants out of the pots for planting, a good deal of care is needed. They should be turned out with the ball of soil intact.

The ball is then placed in the hole and carefully pressed, taking care not to overdo the pressing, a mistake often made by those who are anxious for the care of their plants.

CHAPTER IV

POTS AND BOXES

IN the case of very early crops, the plants are as a rule grown in pots. Sometimes also for one reason or another the main crop is grown in pots, and although this is not the most satisfactory way, special circumstances do at times render it necessary.

The pots used for the purpose should be clean and drainage must be attended to. The compost used must be of the best, but after planting there should be a rather big space from the top of the pot to the top of the compost in order to allow for top dressing, which is essential.

Pots in the case of early crops should not be allowed to stand upon soil in the border, or the roots of the plants will find their way through, and this is not desirable. The pots should therefore stand upon slates or tiles.

22   *Tomato Growing for Profit*

Usually the plants are stopped at about the fourth truss, as this is considered to be a help to the early ripening of the fruits.

If it is necessary to grow the main crop in pots, rather different treatment will be necessary. The holes in the pots should be enlarged for the special purpose of allowing the roots to run through these, and the pots with plants should stand upon the soil, so that the roots may find nourishment beneath the pots.

Whether for early or main crop, it is important that the pots should be of large size. The bigger the better. The pots used should certainly not be less than ten inches across ; if they are bigger than this, so much the better.

It should be remembered that plants in pots will need more watering than will plants grown in the border, although too much water should not be given at first. It is also important that when plants reach the pots in which they are to remain, the soil should be pressed very firmly round the plants. Firm planting is, in fact, always essential.

Actually if they are obtainable large boxes are to be preferred to pots if it is necessary to grow the plants in this way.

A comparatively new method is to grow them in specially made cardboard sink-pots which have no bottoms. The plants are grown above the soil, but their roots have free play in the soil, and it is an easy matter to keep the soil at the right temperature.

Tomato Growing for Profit

At the same time there are ample facilities for the use of the best possible compost and feeding material to do the plants the greatest amount of good.

It is early yet to say whether this method is likely to become generally popular, but up to the present it has met with a good reception.

CHAPTER V

CARE AFTER PLANTING

IT should not be necessary to water the plants for some time after planting.

The method of supporting the plants varies a good deal. There are at least half a dozen methods largely used, bamboo cane supports being one method. The use of soft jute cord is, however, the method most widely used.

Whatever method is employed, however, the same purpose is served.

It will be necessary to keep the plants to a single stem. This is done by pinching out side shoots as soon as they show themselves. Grown in a border it is usual to stop the plants after the fifth truss, allowing one leaf beyond the truss. There are growers, however, who allow their plants more freedom, stopping them only when they reach the top of the house. This method has, however, nothing to recommend it.

Ventilation is an important point, and the care

24 *Tomato Growing for Profit*

with which air is admitted will play an important part in the successful production of a crop.

Weather conditions will largely decide the amount of ventilation that may with safety be allowed.

Caution is necessary for a time after planting, but this does not mean that the ventilators are to be kept tightly closed.

A little air should be admitted right from the start, taking care that the plants are not subject to direct cold draughts, the amount being gradually increased.

More air should be admitted during bright warm days than during cold weather, but it is important that the air should be fresh and moving and not stagnant and foul.

Given care, the amount of air that may be admitted should be the greatest amount possible without danger of injury to the plants.

MULCHING

There is a difference of opinion as to the value of mulching. In some cases this gives definitely improved results, in other cases its value is not so certain. As a matter of fact the difference in results is most likely due to the difference in the kind of soil. Mulching in the case of light soil will without doubt prove of value; in the case of heavy soils its action is not so certain.

A point of great importance is that the manure used for mulching should be thoroughly clean. It

Tomato Growing for Profit

25

is better to let the plants go without the mulch than to use manure which is not clean.

Long straw manure should be used, and it should be spread in the open air a day or two before use. The best time to apply the mulch is after the first truss of fruit is set, although some growers prefer to apply two or three light mulchings.

A mulch of this kind assists to conserve moisture and also helps to feed the plants.

TRIMMING

The removal of a part of the foliage of tomatoes is, although generally practised, an operation that is little understood. Too severe thinning is the most common mistake. The reason for trimming is to allow a full supply of light and air to circulate round the trusses. To strip the plants of the greater part of their foliage is to defeat the object for which the work has been carried out.

If the leaves are healthy they will help to feed the fruit trusses, and by removing them the trusses will suffer.

Lower leaves that are resting on or are near the ground and are partly decayed should be trimmed off, as should other leaves that are preventing light and air reaching the tomatoes.

It is best also to do such trimming as is necessary in two or three operations and not to rob the plant of any great amount of foliage at once. The whole operation is a commonsense one, and the grower

26 *Tomato Growing for Profit*

who removes such foliage as is necessary and no more will benefit by improved crops.

Trimmings should always be taken out of the house and burned at once.

WEIGHT OF CROP

There are some very mistaken ideas in existence as to the quantity of fruit a plant may be expected to produce. Every plant should do its share, but the particularly heavy yields sometimes mentioned are the exception if they exist at all, and the grower would be wise not to take too much notice of statements of this kind.

A really good yield per plant is about seven pounds. This is perhaps slightly above an average, but it is not beyond a possible yield and should be the aim of the grower. At the same time it should be remembered that a smaller yield of really high-grade tomatoes will bring a bigger return than will a heavy yield, a big proportion of which consists of low-grade fruit.

The first efforts of the grower should be directed towards tomatoes of excellent quality, and having done all in one's power to ensure this, the second consideration should be that of a heavy yield. It is better to sacrifice a part of the weight of the crop rather than that the quality should suffer.

Tomato Growing for Profit **27**

CHAPTER VI

GATHERING AND MARKETING

TOMATOES should be picked with the stalk. The actual stage of ripeness at which the fruit should be gathered will depend upon several factors, one of the most important of which is the weather conditions at the time of harvesting.

If the weather is cool and dull the tomatoes may be allowed to become almost ripe before being picked, but if very hot weather prevails they should be gathered before they have changed to the full red colour; as far as is possible fruit of the same grade and in the same package should be evenly coloured.

Early and late crops may be allowed to approach the ripe stage before gathering, but the main crop should as a rule be picked earlier.

Picking in the cool of the day is preferable when the weather is hot, but is not so important during cool weather.

Markets vary to some extent in their preferences and it should be the aim of the grower to supply the market with tomatoes in the condition in which they are most in demand.

GRADING

The method of grading tomatoes has been brought to a higher pitch of perfection than is the case with many of the products of the land. The method of distinguishing between the grades is

28 *Tomato Growing for Profit*

simple, the colour of the packing paper telling at a glance the quality of the grade.

It is true that the standard of grade depends to some extent upon the grower, and that now and again a grower will send as top grade, tomatoes which other growers would relegate to a lower position. This happens more frequently when good quality tomatoes are scarce, but on the whole growers realise the importance of careful grading and the standard is well maintained.

Tomatoes may be packed under the National Mark, in which case the standard is definitely fixed and must be rigidly adhered to. Particulars of the pack should be obtained from the Ministry of Agriculture.

There is no doubt that the grower who packs under the National Mark reaps a certain benefit from doing so. This method of packing is becoming increasingly popular with the public, and as a result with salesmen, and growers who are able to comply with the conditions of packing under this scheme would be wise to give it consideration.

Tomatoes may be packed in standard boxes or half-boxes. The boxes hold twelve pounds of fruit and the half-boxes six pounds; in chip baskets with handles to hold twelve pounds and six pounds, in veneer boxes to hold twelve pounds and six; in the strike which holds twelve pounds and in the six-pound wicker handle basket. Now and again also punnets are used.

Tomato Growing for Profit 29

Apart from the National Mark the packages most generally used are as follows, packed with pink paper. Tomatoes averaging five or six to the pound, almost equal in size and of good colour, round and firm and free from blemish.

Pink and White from six to nine to the pound, with other qualities equal to the Pink.

Blue from five to nine to the pound, quality the same as for the Pink, except that the colour need not be perfect.

White includes both extra large and very small; the fruit is sound but may be blemished and need not be of such good shape.

There is also a Blue and White pack consisting of very small fruits.

Machines are available for grading, but these are more largely used in the tomato exporting countries than they are here. Where there are large quantities of tomatoes to be graded there is no doubt that a grading machine will be a useful acquisition, but with smaller growers grading by eye is likely still to continue. Many growers are experts at grading without the use of machinery.

PACKING

A certain amount of experience is needed before one can become an expert at packing. It is advisable to allow the same employees, men or women, to do the packing year after year, as by so doing one is assured of a uniform pack, and salesmen quickly

30 *Tomato Growing for Profit*

get to know that they can rely upon the tomatoes being packed up to standard. If constant changes are made in the packers, the quality of the pack will vary a good deal and little or no dependence can be placed upon its uniformity.

Thick paper is used over the bottom and round the sides of strikes and similar packages to prevent injury to the tomatoes.

For box packing and for chips, wood wool will be necessary.

In packing, every package that has been previously used should be thoroughly cleaned, as should also the packing shed and shelf. It is impossible to overdo cleanliness with tomatoes.

Apart from the National Mark, many growers have their own special label, which serves a very useful purpose in getting their produce known.

CHAPTER VII

DISEASES OF TOMATOES

THE grower who is able to keep his plants free from pests and diseases has gone the greater part of the way towards success. Unfortunately this is an ideal not possible of attainment. All that is possible is to reduce these troubles to a minimum, and this can only be done by thorough cultivation and by a careful and constant watch so that any trouble showing itself may be at once dealt with.

Tomato Growing for Profit

SLEEPY SICKNESS

Sleepy Sickness of tomatoes is at times the cause of serious loss to growers, and unfortunately there is no real remedy. It has been found, however, that the sickness is less serious in a high temperature than is the case when the temperature is low.

When there are any signs of this disease, therefore, the temperature should be at once raised for a time.

Usually the disease makes its first appearance about the second week in April.

The signs of disease are a sudden wilting of the plant, and although there may be less serious reasons for plants wilting in a similar manner, where such wilting is noticed the plants should always be looked upon with suspicion until the real cause has been discovered.

In addition to raising the temperature of the house for a time it will be desirable to withhold water, apart from the fact that the atmosphere should be kept in a moist condition.

A top dressing of soil in order to encourage the formation of new roots will prove of great assistance.

Dying and dead plants should be dug up and at once burned so that the spread of the disease from this source is prevented.

The soil should be thoroughly sterilised before a new crop of tomatoes is grown in an affected house.

32 *Tomato Growing for Profit*

" STRIPE "

This disease is found most commonly in houses in which too much nitrogen and not sufficient potash has been fed to the plants. It is essential that a sufficiency of potash should be available, and where this is the case there is less likely to be loss from this cause.

If " stripe " should make its appearance in a house of tomatoes, it is very important that affected plants should not be handled for any necessary work before healthy plants are handled. The greatest care should be taken to avoid carrying the disease from unhealthy plants to those that have escaped, and with this end in view the most careful cleanliness should be observed, once the disease has appeared.

It should be the aim of the grower, by seeing that the plants have available a sufficiency of potash and by looking after the general health of the plants in every possible way, to prevent the appearance of " stripe," but once the disease has made its appearance, it should be confined within as narrow limits as possible.

MOSAIC DISEASE

This disease is important in many ways, but it is particularly serious from the point of view of the grower, because the disease may be carried through the seed from one generation to the next. For this reason it is never wise to save the seed from a

Tomato Growing for Profit 33

house in which any of the plants are affected with mosaic. It is indeed essential that seed for planting should be obtained from houses quite free from this trouble.

The disease affects mostly the leaves, but fruit is not free from attack. The greatest care should be taken that when at work among the plants the disease is not taken from a plant already affected to a healthy plant; unless the greatest care is exercised this will often occur.

The mottled appearance sometimes seen on leaves and fruit is a sign of the presence of mosaic.

DAMPING OFF

This is a disease which attacks seedlings, affecting the stems of these just above soil level. The trouble is due to a fungus in the soil which is encouraged by excessive moisture and also by over-crowding. If these are avoided there is much less danger of loss from this cause.

The Ministry of Agriculture in their leaflet on Tomato Culture state that when damping off first appears it is possible to check its further spread by the use of a solution of Cheshunt Compound. This is made by crushing eleven parts by weight of fresh ammonium carbonate (sal volatile) to a fine powder, thoroughly mixing it with two parts by weight of powdered copper sulphate, and storing the mixture for about twenty-four hours in a tightly-corked glass or stoneware jar. The solution used

C

for watering the plants is then prepared by dissolving one ounce of the dry mixture in a little hot water and making up to two gallons. This should not be done in iron, tin or zinc vessels.

If soil in which diseased seedlings have been growing is needed again for the same purpose, it must be sterilised by one of the methods already mentioned before being again used.

TOMATO LEAF RUST OR MILDEW

Although mildew is not the proper name for the disease, it is given here as it is so commonly used.

Tomato Leaf Rust or Mildew.

At first this disease shows itself in the form of pale yellow patches on the upper sides of young leaflets. These patches gradually get bigger. Patches of the same kind develop on the under surface of the leaflets.

The stems also become affected with rusty or blackish marks, and at times the fruit is also attacked.

This is a dangerous disease in that, unless steps are taken to deal with it as soon as it appears, it will very rapidly spread and often ruin the whole crop.

Tomato Growing for Profit 35

Prevention is better than cure, and the chief methods of prevention in this case consist in the avoidance of over-watering and the careful regulation of the temperature so that there is no sudden rise or fall. Careful stoking will see to this.

Affected leaves should be collected and burned, as should also whole plants where these are sufficiently badly attacked to warrant this drastic treatment.

The fungus which is responsible for this disease is known as *Cladosporium fulvum*.

ROOT ROT

Many of the diseases of the tomato may be prevented or are little likely to occur if the advice given as to soil sterilisation is carried out; this is one of the diseases which generally shows itself when there has been neglect in this direction. After its appearance the soil should always be sterilised before a new crop.

BOTRYTIS

This disease attacks both the fruits and the stems of the plants. It is one of the few diseases not affected by soil sterilisation, attacking just as seriously plants grown in sterilised soil as those grown in soil that is not sterilised.

In order to prevent the appearance of this trouble, which may be responsible for a good deal of loss to growers, the greatest care should be taken with

36 *Tomato Growing for Profit*

watering and ventilation. Where these are carefully carried out there is much less danger of attack than is the case when these two operations have been neglected.

Attacked parts of plants should be cut cleanly away and at once burned.

If the disease becomes serious, spraying may be carried out with a two per cent. solution of Calcium Bisulphite with beneficial effect to the plants.

BLOSSOM END ROT

May cause a certain loss of fruit, but it can be prevented if watering is carefully attended to. In almost every case the first appearance of this disease may be traced to an irregular water supply.

BLIGHT

There is a blight which attacks tomato plants which is closely connected with the serious trouble that has faced potato growers during the last few years. Dark purplish spots first show themselves on the bottom leaves and later brown spots on the fruit.

If the disease is serious, plants and fruits that are badly affected should be burnt. If it is carried out sufficiently early, spraying with Burgundy mixture will check the disease and prevent its spread, but to be effective this must be done at the first sign of the trouble.

CHAPTER VIII

PESTS

SOIL pests are among the most serious with which the tomato grower has to contend. These include Wireworms, Leather Jackets, Millepedes and Slugs as well as the Root Knot Eelworm. It would be as well, therefore, to deal with these first.

It is chiefly in new houses, where the soil is already infested with wireworm, that trouble will be experienced from these pests. If they are thought to be present, naphthalene should be worked into the soil before any planting is done. It will be necessary to well water this into the ground. The rate of application should be equal to two ounces per square yard. Naphthalene is recommended here because it is harmless to plant life; many other soil insecticides, while effective from the point of view of killing the pest, are not harmless to plants, and if used at all must be used some time before any planting is done.

It is fairly easy to trap wireworms in tomato houses because there are many vegetables that they prefer to tomatoes. Pieces of carrot are excellent for this purpose; a pointed stick is stuck in the carrot, which is then buried to a depth of two or three inches beneath the soil. These traps should be examined from time to time and such wireworms as are caught should be destroyed.

LEATHER JACKETS

Leather Jackets are somewhat more difficult to deal with than are wireworms, but here again naphthalene worked into the ground in the same way as for wireworm will be particularly beneficial. If these pests are present in any quantity it will be advisable to get rid of them before planting, so that a good beginning may be made.

MILLEPEDES

Millepedes may be trapped by placing beneath the soil mangolds or beets with pointed stick attached in the same way that wireworms are caught. Naphthalene is also a useful remedy for these pests when used in the same way as previously described.

SLUGS

If slugs prove at all troublesome they may be dealt with either by such substances as powdered coke, which the slugs do not like, or by traps such as moist oatmeal; heaps of bran, mash or cabbage and lettuce leaves will attract the pests, which should then be destroyed.

ROOT KNOT EELWORM

This pest bores into the roots of tomatoes and causes galls to appear. The leaves turn yellow and have an unhealthy appearance and the plants become very weak and unable to produce a full crop. This

Tomato Growing for Profit 39

pest scarcely ever appears in properly sterilised soil, and both the prevention and cure of eelworm is to carefully sterilise the soil.

Among other pests of the tomatoes apart from those connected with the soil are one or two which may at times be responsible for very serious damage to the crop.

THE TOMATO MOTH

Although the methods of dealing with this pest are much more effective than was the case a few years ago, it is still at times responsible for considerable loss to growers. The moths are brown with pale markings, the caterpillars vary to some extent in colour from greenish and brownish to yellow. Both the leaves and young fruits are attacked.

Spraying with arsenate of lead at the rate of four pounds of paste to each hundred gallons of water will kill the pest, but as this is a poisonous wash it must on no account be used within six weeks of picking the fruit.

Hand-picking leaves on which eggs are found is often practised, as is also the use of traps of two kinds. The first consists of old pieces of sacking. These should be loosely folded and placed on the pipes under gutters and on lower wires. Every third week the sacks should be collected and dipped for about a minute or so in boiling water and then shaken out, when it will be found that many other

40 *Tomato Growing for Profit*

pests beside the Tomato Moth caterpillar have been captured and destroyed.

In trapping the moth two-pound jam jars will be needed. Into each of these jars three ounces of a mixture made up as follows should be placed. One part of thick brown treacle, two parts of good ale and one per cent. sodium fluoride. The sodium fluoride should be added after the treacle and beer are in the bottles. Sufficient of this to cover a sixpenny-piece will be about the right amount for each jar.

It is important that the jars should have a rather wide mouth, be fairly deep and have a definite shoulder. If these facts are remembered the jars may be either larger or smaller than those mentioned, using proportionate numbers per house.

The number needed of the size given will be three jars to each hundred-foot house. The jars are tied to the wires an even distance apart. They will need examining, their contents emptying and refilling three or four times during the season. This should be done at regular intervals.

It is a safeguard also to keep the same picking baskets for work in the houses. It is perhaps not an uncommon occurrence for this pest to be introduced through taking strikes or baskets which have been in houses and districts where the pest is prevalent into houses which up to that time have been clear of the trouble. The wickerwork is a good place for chrysalides.

WHITE FLY

This is a common and troublesome pest of tomatoes, which, like the tomato moth, may be the cause of a good deal of loss to growers. Fortunately there are effective methods of control which should be used.

Fumigation is the only effective remedy, and it

Tomato affected by White Fly attack.

will be necessary to carry through this operation twice in order to be effective. The material used for the purpose is a very deadly poison and the greatest care will be necessary in using it. The first precaution to be observed is to leave the house at once after preparations have been completed, and the second is not to enter the house for at least two or three hours after the door or doors have been allowed to remain wide open the following morning.

42 *Tomato Growing for Profit*

The operation is known as Cyaniding and should be carried out after sunset on a quiet night.

A number of jars will be needed for the purpose, in each of which is placed three ounces of water first, and secondly one and a half ounces (fluid) of sulphuric acid added carefully and slowly. These jars should be placed evenly down the house. The cyanide is evenly weighed out in ounces on a piece of paper, and this quantity is placed by the side of each jar.

Plants should be on the dry side and no heat should be given unless there is danger of a very cold night.

The man doing the work walks from the far end towards the door. If the houses are in blocks, all must start at the same time and walk quickly, tipping the cyanide into each jar as they reach it. The ventilators should be closed tightly before this is done, and as soon as the men are outside the door is closed and locked.

The door should not be opened until the following morning and the house should not be entered until, as previously stated, the door has been left wide open for some time.

A second fumigation should be performed from fourteen to twenty-five days after the first according to weather conditions. In hot weather the shorter time and in cool weather the longer period.

The cyanide may be purchased in safety tins or ready packed in ounce packages, in which case it should be kept in air-tight tins. As it is very

Tomato Growing for Profit 43

poisonous stuff to handle, the safety-tin method is the best, but it is always advisable to purchase it in one of these forms.

The amount needed per house will vary with the width, height and length of the house, but it may be taken as a safe guide that from one-fifth to one-quarter ounce should be used for every thousand cubic feet.

Jars should be thoroughly cleansed after use.

RED SPIDER

This is one of the most serious pests with which the tomato grower has to deal.

Careful selection of varieties will do something towards preventing the appearance of this pest.

The Red Spider flourishes most freely in a dry atmosphere, and the most effective way of preventing its appearance and of eradicating it once it has appeared is by use of the syringe, so that, without giving sufficient water to injure the crop, the atmosphere is in a sufficiently moist condition to prevent the spread of this pest.

Sulphur may also be used sprinkled on the hot-water pipes when these are not above the heat at which the hand may with comfort be placed upon them.

If the pipes are hotter than this it will be unsafe to use the sulphur, as fumes which may seriously injure the plants will be given off, and reliance will have to be placed solely upon the syringe.

Tomato Growing for Profit

THRIPS

This is another pest which is at times trouble-some to tomatoes ; the prevention and remedy is by means of sufficient moisture, and the remarks made on the treatment for Red Spider, by means of the syringe, will be equally effective in the case of this pest.

APHIDES

Green-fly and other forms of sucking insects are usually controlled by fumigation with nicotine. This should be used according to directions.

CUCUMBERS

CHAPTER IX

SITE

THE commercial cultivation of cucumbers, like that of tomatoes, is an important industry and one which is extending rapidly.

Cucumbers and tomatoes are at times grown in the same type of house by the same grower, but this is not the best method. The aeroplane type with a high gutter is one of the most suitable types for tomatoes, but a low house is preferable for cucumbers, a favourite type being about fourteen feet in width with walls three to four feet high and ridge eight or nine feet in height.

It is sometimes recommended that the site chosen should have a gentle slope towards the south, and while this may have a good deal to recommend it, we much prefer a level surface, because of the greater ease of getting an even temperature, and even moisture, both as regards atmosphere and soil.

As a rule, however, the grower has to be content with such land as is available for the purpose, and it is comforting to realise the wide variety of sites and conditions under which cucumbers can be successfully grown.

46 *Cucumber Growing for Profit*

The piping of the houses is a matter of some importance. Overhead pipes are not the most suitable for cucumbers, the pipes being best at ground level.

Thorough drainage is essential with cucumbers. It is almost useless to hope for success if the drainage system is at fault whether this is natural or artificial.

The maximum amount of light should be available for the houses. This is also an important consideration.

It should be remembered that continuance of growth is one of the main objects which the cucumber grower has in view. If the plants receive a serious check at any stage of their growth it will prove fatal to the success of the crop. It is for this reason that thorough control of temperature and moisture are such important factors towards success.

PROPAGATION

The usual method of propagation is from seed. Cuttings for one reason or another, although occasionally used, are not generally considered a commercial proposition and this method has almost entirely gone out of practice.

Seed is usually sown in shallow trays. Sifted soil is used to cover the seed. Ordinary seed trays are the most useful for the purpose, but any trays of convenient size may be used providing they are thoroughly cleansed before use. The best soil

Cucumber Growing for Profit 47

with which to fill the seed trays is a light friable loam.

Pots are not often used on a commercial scale, although there is no doubt that for the grower who can give time and attention to the work, planting the seed one to each 60 pot will have many advantages.

For cucumbers grown on a commercial scale a propagating house is almost a necessity. This, like the tomato and the cucumber houses, should be kept thoroughly clean everywhere, and if at all possible the soil used in the seed trays should be sterilised.

Moisture in the atmosphere is just as essential as is keeping a correct temperature. This should be maintained at between 65 and 75 degrees, although some growers claim to obtain good results with a temperature sinking at times as low as 60 degrees We do not think it advisable to go as low as this.

The period during which the seed is sown will vary with the time that it is intended to gather the crop, as well as with the situation of the houses. A favourite time for the work to be done with commercial growers is during the last week of the old year or the first week of the new year, although in very favoured positions seed is sown earlier than this. This may be taken as a suitable time for putting in seed for a main crop of cucumbers.

If planted in boxes the seed would be transferred to small pots, usually 60's, after about a week, and

Cucumber Growing for Profit

from these in about ten days to 48's. Some growers transfer from boxes straight into 48's. It is largely a matter of opinion which method is the better.

VARIETIES

There are three or four varieties largely grown commercially. They include the Telegraph, Butcher's Disease Resister and Rochford's Improved Favourite. Whatever variety is chosen, the greatest care should be taken as to the source from which the seed is obtained. It is important that this should be obtained from houses altogether free from disease.

CHAPTER X

PREPARATION AND PLANTING,
CLEANING

IT is essential that the houses should be thoroughly cleaned after the old crop has been removed and before the new crop is planted.

A thorough scrubbing down is almost essential and is by no means a waste of time. Paraffin soap is perhaps one of the most effective materials for washing down houses at this time to ensure thorough cleanliness.

The soil should be sterilised either by chemicals or steam, and in any case steam sterilisation should be employed from time to time, although it is not necessary each year.

Cucumber Growing for Profit   49

Spraying with cresylic acid emulsion is essential between crops. This should be prepared and used exactly according to directions.

Lime is useful at this time; the walls may be lime-washed and the whole of the base of the house may be given a dressing of lime.

PREPARING THE BEDS AND PLANTING

Cucumbers are usually grown on raised beds or mounds. In some districts the raised beds run the whole length of the houses. In other districts mounds are preferred. Success will follow either method if the preparation has been thorough.

Unless one is an experienced grower it is as well not to try experiments with the compost used, but to mix this from materials that have previously been well tried and have proved suitable for the purpose. A good compost may be obtained by mixing two parts of good loam to one of dung.

It is important that a sour loam should not be employed for the purpose, neither should a sticky clay or a poor sand or chalk soil.

The soil in the beds should be warm before the plants are brought in. For this reason the beds or mounds should be made up a short time before they will be needed.

It is important that the plants should receive no check when being moved from the propagating house to their permanent quarters, and if necessary protection should be provided.

D

50 *Cucumber Growing for Profit*

The most suitable distance apart for the plants will vary with the variety, but different growers have different opinions as to the most suitable distances at which it is advisable to plant. It may be taken as a safe guide that from one and a half to two and a half feet apart, according to the vigour of the variety, will be correct, although thirty inches will only be necessary in the case of very vigorous plants.

As to the most suitable method of making the holes, we repeat here what we wrote in the section devoted to Tomatoes. This is not of much importance so long as the holes are carefully and properly made. Dibbers are very largely employed for the purpose as being convenient and they answer well.

Whatever method is employed, the holes should be made before the plants are brought into the house, and the plants in their pots should be allowed to stand in the holes for about two days before being planted.

In planting, the plants should be carefully turned out of their pots with the ball of soil intact and should be carefully pressed into position just below the surface of the surrounding soil.

A thorough watering should be given immediately after planting.

If the plants have been planted out under favourable conditions they will grow very quickly, and if they do not do so, it may be taken for granted

Cucumber Growing for Profit   51

that there has been an error somewhere. A careful watch should be kept upon the plants in order to minimise as much as possible the resulting check to growth or serious loss may result.

CHAPTER XI

CARE AFTER PLANTING

As soon as the plants are in the beds a careful watch will need to be kept both upon the supply of moisture and upon the temperature.

The cucumber thrives and produces its best crops in a warm moist atmosphere. It will be the aim of the grower to give it these conditions.

The right temperature should be maintained between 65 and 75 degrees. It is true that some growers allow it to fall a little below this, but there is danger in doing so. As near 67 as possible should be the aim of the grower. There will then be little danger of chills destroying the prospects of a full crop.

The amount of water necessary will depend largely upon weather conditions. The cucumber will benefit by a plentiful supply of water, but it can be overdone. In bright warm weather it may be necessary to water every day; in cooler weather every other day will be sufficient.

The Ministry of Agriculture in the leaflet issued on the cultivation of the cucumber give the amount under ordinary conditions as about a gallon and a

52 *Cucumber Growing for Profit*

quarter to each plant every other day applied in one watering. This may be taken as a guide, the amount being varied as weather and other conditions vary.

During spells of very hot sunny weather it will be necessary to shade the glass. This is best done by the usual method of lime-washing it.

Not less important than keeping at a correct temperature and careful watering is that of syringing or damping down as it is termed. In the first place, the control of that pest of the cucumber as well as other glasshouse plants, the Red Spider, depends largely upon the amount of moisture in the atmosphere. In the second place, a moist atmosphere is essential if the cucumber is to thrive and to produce an average crop.

It is usually necessary to syringe from once to three times a day according to weather conditions. In hot weather three times, in warm weather twice, and in cold weather, such as is particularly likely for early crops, once. The syringing or damping down should take the form of a fine spray.

In the case of cucumbers it is not advisable to ventilate the houses at least until the warm weather arrives, and then ventilation should be only in moderation, the ventilators being opened only a mere inch or two for an hour or so at a time. In this respect cucumbers differ from tomatoes. These like free ventilation, the cucumber little or none.

TRIMMING, TRAINING AND STOPPING

Cucumbers are usually allowed to reach the top of the house before being stopped. Laterals are stopped at the first or second joint, except those at the bottom of the plant, which are removed altogether. Sub-laterals, should they appear, are stopped at the first leaf.

In dealing with thinning out of the foliage a good

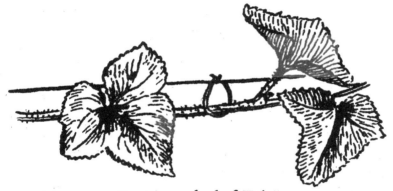

Correct method of Tying.

deal of judgment will be necessary. Leaves which are turning yellow should be removed, and where the foliage is too thick it should be thinned sufficiently to allow the free admission of light and air; more than this is not necessary.

When the plants begin to flower it will be found that two kinds of flowers are produced, male and female. It is important that every male flower should be removed before it has had any opportunity to fertilise, as where this takes place the yield is

54 *Cucumber Growing for Profit*

reduced to a considerable extent and the cucumbers will be less valuable from the market point of view.

Tying is rather a matter of experience, but the plants should be so arranged that they get the greatest value from light and air. If at all possible it is best to allow an employee with some experience to do this work, although a big amount of experience is not important if care in doing the work is exercised.

CHAPTER XII

GATHERING AND MARKETING

CUCUMBERS should be carefully gathered and handled. It is essential that they should arrive at the market in the best possible condition, and in order that this should be the case a good deal of care is necessary.

Grading is important. It is the duty of the grower who wishes to maintain a good connection on the market and to receive satisfactory returns to grade well up to standard. The grower who does this will find his cucumbers are always in demand, and that his special label, if he has one, is asked for by customers of the salesman he supplies.

Cucumbers may be marketed under the National Mark, which is a guarantee of a certain standard, and growers who desire to market under this scheme will be able to obtain all the necessary information from the Ministry of Agriculture. The scheme has

Cucumber Growing for Profit

proved a success and without doubt it is of benefit to the industry.

There are growers, however, who for one reason or another do not adopt this method of packing cucumbers, and where this is the case it is useful to have one's own label, so that a grower's packages will be known by this. If the cucumbers are well packed this will be a big advantage.

Cucumbers packed in Trays.

The usual types of packages used for cucumbers are—

The Cucumber Box, made to hold two layers of from fifteen to thirty cucumbers weighing not less than eighteen pounds.

The Single Layer Tray, containing from eight to fifteen cucumbers weighing from seven to nine pounds.

The Wicker Flat, containing from thirty to sixty

56 *Cucumber Growing for Profit*

cucumbers the weight of which is thirty-six pounds. Hay is usually used to prevent the cucumbers being damaged, a thin layer being placed on the bottom of the flats. Blue paper is almost always used with cucumbers, being placed between the layers in flats.

Careful packing means tight packing, and tight packing is essential if the cucumbers are to arrive on the market in first-class condition.

Naturally both the supply and demand are restricted during the winter months, and a smaller package is therefore more useful from the market point of view during this period, and it is for those growers marketing at this time that the single layer flat is most useful.

With cucumbers as with tomatoes it is a good plan so far as is possible to keep the same employees for packing right through. Some will prove more competent than others, and by giving reliable graders and packers the work, the grower will know that his produce will reach the market in the best possible condition and that his reputation will be maintained on the market.

CHAPTER XIII

PESTS AND DISEASES

THE chief pests of the cucumber are the Root Knot Eelworm, Wireworm, Thrips and Aphides. These also attack the tomato, and the method of

Cucumber Growing for Profit

dealing with them is similar. The grower is referred to Chapter VIII, where they are fully dealt with. Naphthalene fumigation will destroy Red Spider in cucumber houses. About five in the

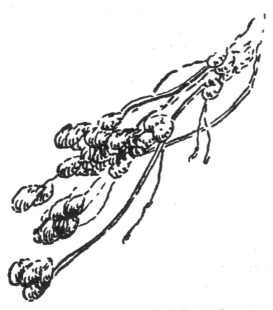

Cucumber Roots attacked by Eelworm.

afternoon flaked naphthalene is sifted through a sieve, 16 meshes to the inch, on to beds that have been well watered. Six pounds to a hundred-foot house should be used, with the temperature not less than 74° F.

MILDEW

Powdery Mildew attacks cucumbers from time to time. There is another and more serious type of mildew which attacks the crop in some countries, but from which we have so far remained free.

58 *Cucumber Growing for Profit*

Where this disease is present the plants should be dusted with sulphur. This is not a cure for the trouble, but it is a method of preventing its spread. It is therefore important that the dusting should be carried out before the disease becomes at all serious.

LEAF SPOT

Several forms of disease of cucumbers have been given the name Leaf Spot. Excessive moisture in the atmosphere and sudden changes of temperature are largely responsible for the appearance of these diseases. The matter of the control of moisture is perhaps somewhat more difficult than is the control of temperature, as cucumbers must have a certain amount of moisture. Care should, however, be exercised not to overdo the syringing where any sign of Leaf Spot in any of its forms is present.

Colletotrichum oligochætum and *Cladosporium cucumerinum* are two of the most serious forms of the Leaf Spot. The first of these usually shows itself during the spring in the form of reddish spots on the leaves, which spread until the leaves die.

It is important that all affected parts of plants should be cut away at once and destroyed by burning. It should be remembered that the disease may be carried from plant to plant by the clothes of the worker as well as by other means, so that prompt action is always necessary.

Spraying with liver of sulphur and flour paste is

Cucumber Growing for Profit 59

the most effective means of control, although a sprinkling of powdered sulphur will also be useful in retarding the spread of the disease.

In the case of the second form of Leaf Spot mentioned the spots are present in large numbers and are light brown in colour. Dusting with sulphur should also be carried out, and in this case also all attacked parts of plants should at once be removed and burnt. This disease is responsible for Gummosis. Liver of sulphur and flour paste are also useful in the case of this disease.

WILT

There are two forms of Wilt which may at times attack cucumbers and a third form which is fortunately much more rare.

Fusarium wilt attacks the plants when the soil temperature is high. There is no cure, but affected plants as well as the soil in which these are grown should be removed. Fresh soil mixed with lime should replace this, and before any planting is done this should be watered with Cheshunt Compound.

Verticillium wilt spreads most rapidly when the temperature is comparatively low and there is overabundant moisture. The temperature should be raised to above 70 degrees and watering should be reduced.

Bacterial wilt is the most uncommon. It is carried from plant to plant by insects. The temperature both day and night should be raised

60   *Cucumber Growing for Profit*

considerably until it is at least ninety degrees in order to check this trouble.

MOSAIC DISEASE

This sometimes attacks cucumbers and is spread through the agency of green-fly. There is no remedy, but in order to prevent the spread of this trouble every effort should be made to keep the houses clear of sucking insects, while drainage may also receive attention.

CHAPTER XIV
OUTDOOR TOMATOES AND RIDGE CUCUMBERS
TOMATOES

No work of this kind would be complete without some reference to the outdoor cultivation of tomatoes and cucumbers.

It is true that only in very limited areas are climatic conditions suitable for raising tomatoes out of doors, but they are grown commercially on a sufficiently large scale in these districts to warrant their inclusion here.

Weather vagaries make the risk of loss considerably greater with tomatoes grown out of doors than is the case when they have the protection of glass, but by careful cultivation this risk may be greatly reduced.

The plants are raised on a mild hot-bed; the

Cucumber Growing for Profit 61

seed being sown in boxes, taking care that there are holes in the bottom of the boxes to admit of drainage. These will need the protection of lights, which are best at first covered with mats. Only a little ventilation should be admitted when the weather is warm. The seed should be sown early in March.

About three weeks or a month later, when the young plants have two rough leaves, they are planted in other boxes two inches apart each way. These are again placed in frames on a mild hot-bed.

A further transplanting takes place to four inches apart each way about a month later.

Some growers dispense with one of these transfers, but it is not advisable to do so.

No hot-bed is needed at this stage, but protection from frost will be necessary.

Planting out should be done in June as soon as weather conditions are suitable, but not earlier than this. Care should be taken to give plenty of room for development, and the plants should be moved with care so that no check is received when they are put out. This is particularly important.

Supports should be provided either by means of wires stretched along the rows or by stakes, and tying and trimming should receive attention.

The plants are usually stopped early in August.

There are a number of pests, such as birds, which are sometimes a source of trouble where tomatoes are grown out of doors. Such protection as is possible should be given in this case, and the lower tomatoes removed before they are fully ripe.

RIDGE CUCUMBERS

Where it is possible, as in parts of the south, to grow ridge cucumbers, these may prove a profitable crop. Their flavour is good, quite equal to that of any other class, but their appearance is not usually up to the standard of the indoor product.

Method of providing Ridge Cucumbers with protection at Night, Mats or Calico spread over a Triangular Frame.

A great deal depends, however, upon the methods of cultivation.

During the early stages this is similar to that necessary for an indoor crop; the seed being sown about the second week in April on a hot-bed. Ample ventilation must, however, be given before the plants are planted out.

A trench is taken out about two feet wide and filled in with fermenting manure; this must be well firmed and left for a time. The plants are planted out on the mound thus formed during

Cucumber Growing for Profit 63

May, the rows being six feet apart and the plants about two feet apart or slightly less according to vigour.

Protection should be provided by means of mats or cloches at first, the amount of ventilation being gradually increased until no further protection is needed. Cloches are best, but are more expensive, although they will last for years if carefully handled.

The varieties suitable for this method include King of the Ridge and Best of All Ridge.

The Gherkin is largely grown for pickling.

Printed in the USA
CPSIA information can be obtained
at www.ICGtesting.com
LVHW091256261023
761678LV00043B/38